An Exhc

and Unity

John Bunyan

Alpha Editions

This edition published in 2021

ISBN : 9789355340832

Design and Setting By
Alpha Editions
www.alphaedis.com
Email - info@alphaedis.com

AN EXHORTATION TO PEACE AND UNITY.

[We deem it proper to state, that, though the following Treatise of Christian Union appears in nearly all the collected editions of BUNYAN'S WORKS, yet its genuineness has been called in question by the Rev. Mr Philip in his admirable work, "The Life and Times of Bunyan." Without here entering into this question, we have separately appended it to the works of Bunyan in this volume, and trust that it will not prove unacceptable to our readers, especially considering the efforts that are now being made to promote the living union of all true Christians who hold the one Lord, the one faith, and the one baptism.]

Endeavouring to keep the unity of the Spirit in the bond of peace.—
Ephesians iv. 3.

BELOVED, religion is the great bond of human society; and it were well if itself were kept within the bond of unity; and that it may so be, let us, according to the text, use our utmost endeavours "to keep the unity of the Spirit in the bond of peace."

These words contain a counsel and a caution: the counsel is, That we endeavour the unity of the Spirit; the caution is, That we do it in the bond of peace; as if I should say, I would have you live in unity, but yet I would have you to be careful that you do not purchase unity with the breach of charity.

Let us therefore be cautious that we do not so press after unity in practice and opinion as to break the bond of peace and affection.

In the handling of these words, I shall observe this method.

I. I shall open the sense of the text.

II. I shall shew wherein this unity and peace consist.

III. I shall shew you the fruits and benefits of it, together with nine inconveniences and mischiefs that attend those churches where unity and peace is wanting.

IV. And, lastly, I shall give you twelve directions and motives for the obtaining of it.

1. As touching the sense of the text, when ye are counselled to keep the unity of the Spirit, we are not to understand the Spirit of God, as personally so considered; because the Spirit of God, in that sense, is not capable of being divided, and so there would be no need for us to endeavour to keep the unity of it.

By the unity of the spirit then, we are to understand that unity of mind which the Spirit of God calls for, and requires Christians to endeavour after; hence it is that we are exhorted, by one spirit, with one mind, to strive together for the faith of the gospel; Phil. i. 27.

But farther, the apostle in these words alludes to the state and composition of a natural body, and doth thereby inform us, that the mystical body of Christ holds an analogy with the natural body of man: as, 1. In the natural body there must be a spirit to animate it; for the body without the spirit is dead; James ii. 26. So it is in the mystical body of Christ; the apostle no sooner tells of that one body, but he minds us of that one Spirit; Eph. iv. 4.

2. The body hath joints and hands to unite all the parts; so hath the mystical body of Christ; Col. ii. 19. This is that bond of peace mentioned in the text, as also in the 16th verse of the same chapter, where the whole body is said to be fitly joined together, and compacted, by that which every joint supplieth.

3. The natural body receives counsel and nourishment from the head; so doth the mystical body of Christ; he is their counsellor, and him they must hear; he is their head, and him they must hold: hence it is that the apostle complaineth, Col. ii. 19, of some that did not hold the head from which the whole body by joints and hands hath nourishment.

4. The natural body cannot well subsist, if either the spirit be wounded or the joints broken or dislocated; the body cannot bear a wounded or broken spirit—"A broken spirit drieth the bones;" Prov. xvii. 22, and "A wounded spirit who can bear?" Prov. xviii. 14. And, on the other hand, how often have the disjointing of the body, and the breakings thereof, occasioned the expiration of the spirit? In like manner it fares with the mystical body of Christ; how do divided spirits break the bonds of peace, which are the joints of this body? And how do the breakings of the body and church of Christ wound the spirit of Christians, and oftentimes occasion the spirit and life of Christianity to languish, if not to expire. How needful is it then that we endeavour the unity of the spirit in the bond of peace!

II. I now come to shew you wherein this unity and peace consists; and this I shall demonstrate in five particulars.

1. This unity and peace may consist with the ignorance of many truths, and in the holding of some errors; or else this duty of peace and unity could not be practicable by any on this side perfection: but we must now endeavour the unity of the spirit, till we come to the unity of the faith, and of the knowledge of the Son of God; Eph. iv. 13. Because now, as the apostle saith, "We know in part, and we prophesy in part," and "Now we see through a glass darkly;" 1 Cor. xiii. 9, 12. And as this is true in general, so we may find

it true if we descend to particular instances. The disciples seem to be ignorant of that great truth which they had often, and in much plainness, been taught by their Master once and again, viz., that his kingdom was not of this world, and that in the world they should suffer and be persecuted; yet in the 1st of the Acts, ver. 6, we read, that they asked of him if he would at this time restore the kingdom to Israel? thereby discovering that Christ's kingdom (as they thought) should consist in his temporal jurisdiction over Israel, which they expected should now commence and take place amongst them. Again, our Lord tells them, that he had many things to say (and these were many important truths) which they could not now bear; John xvi. 12. And that these were important truths, appear by the 10th and 11th verses, where he is discoursing of righteousness and judgment, and then adds, that he had yet many things to say which they could not bear; and thereupon promises the Comforter to lead them into ALL TRUTH; which implies, that they were yet ignorant of many truths, and consequently held divers errors; and yet for all this, he prays for, and presses them to, their great duty of peace and unity; John xiv. 27; xvii. 21. To this may be added that of Heb. v. 11, where the author saith, he had many things to say of the priestly office of Christ, which by reason of their dulness they were not capable to receive; as also that in the 10th of the Acts, where Peter seems to be ignorant of the truth, viz., that the gospel was to be preached to all nations; and contrary hereunto, he erred in thinking it unlawful to preach amongst the Gentiles. I shall add two texts more, one in Acts xix., where we read that those disciples which had been discipled and baptized by John were yet ignorant of the Holy Ghost, and knew not (as the text tells us) whether there were any holy Ghost or no; though John did teach constantly, that he that should come after him should baptize with the Holy Ghost and fire. From hence we may easily and plainly infer, that Christians may be ignorant of many truths, by reason of weak and dull capacities, and other such like impediments, even while those truths are with much plainness delivered to them. Again, we read, Heb. v. 13, of some that were unskilful in the word of righteousness, who nevertheless are called babes in Christ, and with whom unity and peace is to be inviolably kept and maintained.

2. As this unity and peace may consist with the ignorance of many truths, and with the holding some errors, so it must consist with (and it cannot consist without) the believing and practising those things which are necessary to salvation and church-communion; and they are, 1st, Believing that Christ the Son of God died for the sins of men. 2d, That whoever believeth ought to be baptized. The third thing essential to this communion, is a holy and a blameless conversation.

(1.) That believing that the Son of God died for the sins of men is necessary to salvation, I prove by these texts, which tell us, that he that doth not believe shall be damned, Mark xvi. 16; John iii. 36; Rom. x. 9.

That it is also necessary to church-communion appears from Matt. xvi. 16–18. Peter having confessed that Christ was the Son of the living God, Christ thereupon assures Peter, that upon this rock, viz., this profession of faith, or this Christ which Peter had confessed, he would build his church, and the gates of hell should not prevail against it. And, 1 Cor. iii. 11, the apostle having told the Corinthians that they were God's building, presently adds, that they could not be built upon any foundation but upon that which was laid, which was Jesus Christ. All which proves, that Christian society is founded upon the profession of Christ; and not only scripture, but the laws of right reason, dictate this, that some rules and orders must be observed for the founding all society, which must be consented to by all that will be of it. Hence it comes to pass, that to own Christ as the Lord and head of Christians is essential to the founding of Christian society.

(2.) The Scriptures have declared, that this faith gives the professors of it a right to baptism, as in the case of the eunuch, Acts viii. When he demanded why he might not be baptized, Philip answered, that if he believed with all his heart, he might. The eunuch thereupon confessing Christ, was baptized.

Now, that baptism is essential to church-communion, I prove from 1 Cor. xii., where we shall find the apostle labouring to prevent an evil use that might be made of spiritual gifts, as thereby to be puffed up, and to think that such as wanted them were not of the body, or to be esteemed members: he thereupon resolves, that whoever did confess Christ, and own him for his head, did it by the Spirit, ver. 3, though they might not have such a visible manifestation of it as others had, and therefore they ought to be owned as members, as appears, ver. 23. And not only because they have called him Lord by the Spirit, but because they have, by the guidance and direction of the same Spirit, been baptized, ver. 13, "For by one Spirit we are all baptized into one body," &c. I need not go about to confute that notion that some of late have had of this text., viz., that the baptism here spoken of is the baptism of the Spirit, because you have not owned and declared that notion as your judgment, but on the contrary, all of you that I have ever conversed with, have declared it to be understood of baptism with water, by the direction of the Spirit: If so, then it follows, that men and women are declared members of Christ's body by baptism, and cannot be by scripture reputed and esteemed so without it; which farther appears from Rom. vi. 5, where men by baptism are said to be "planted" into the likeness of his death and Col. ii. 12, we are said to be "buried with him" by baptism. All which, together with the consent of all Christians (some few in these later times excepted), do prove that baptism is necessary to the initiating persons into the Church of Christ.

(3.) Holiness of life is essential to church-communion, because it seems to be the reason why Christ founded a church in the world, viz., that men might thereby be watched over, and kept from falling; and that if any be overtaken with a fault, he that is spiritual might restore him, that by this means men and women might be preserved without blame to the coming of Christ; and the grace of God teacheth us to deny ungodliness and worldly lusts, and to live soberly and uprightly in this present evil world; Tit. ii. 11, 12. "And let every one that nameth the name of Christ, depart from iniquity;" 2 Tim. ii. 19. And James tells us (speaking of the Christian religion), that "pure religion, and undefiled before God, is this, To visit the fatherless and widows in their affliction, and to keep ourselves unspotted from the world;" James i. 27. From all which (together with many more texts that might be produced) it appears, that an unholy and profane life is inconsistent with Christian religion and society; and that holiness is essential to salvation and church-communion. So that these three things, faith, baptism, and a holy life, as I said before, all churches must agree and unite in, as those things which, when wanting, will destroy their being. And let not any think, that when I say, believing the Son of God died for the sins of men is essential to salvation and church-communion, that I hereby would exclude all other articles of the Christian creed as not necessary; as the belief of the resurrection of the dead, and eternal judgment, &c., which, for want of time, I omit to speak particularly to, and the rather, because I understand this great article of believing the Son of God died for the sins of men is comprehensive of all others, and is that from whence all other articles may easily be inferred.

And here I would not be mistaken, as though I held there was nothing else for Christians to practise, when I say this is all that is requisite to church-communion; for I very well know, that Christ requires many other things of us, after we are members of his body, which, if we knowingly or maliciously refuse, may be the cause, not only of excommunication, but damnation. But yet these are such things as relate to the well-being and not to the being of churches; as laying on of hands in the primitive times upon believers, by which they did receive the gifts of the Spirit: This, I say, was for the increase and edifying of the body, and not that thereby they might become of the body of Christ, for that they were before. And do not think that I believe laying on of hands was no apostolical institution, because I say men are not thereby made members of Christ's body, or because I say that it is not essential to church-communion. Why should I be thought to be against a fire in the chimney, because I say it must not be in the thatch of the house? Consider, then, how pernicious a thing it is to make every doctrine (though true) the bond of communion; this is that which destroys unity, and by this rule all men must be perfect before they can be in peace: for do we not see daily, that as soon as men come to a clearer understanding of the mind of God (to say the best of what they hold), that presently all men are excommunicable, if not damnable, that do not agree with them. Do not some believe and see that to be pride and covetousness, which others do not, because (it may be) they have more narrowly and diligently searched into their duty of these things than others have? What then? Must all men that have not so large acquaintance of their duty herein be excommunicated? Indeed it were to be wished that more moderation in apparel and secular concernments were found among churches: but God forbid, that if they should come short herein, that we should say, as one lately said, that he could not communicate with such a people, because they were proud and superfluous in their apparel.

Let me appeal to such, and demand of them, if there was not a time, since they believed and were baptized, wherein they did not believe laying on of hands a duty? and did they not then believe, and do they not still believe, they were members of the body of Christ? And was not there a time when you did not so well understand the nature and extent of pride and covetousness as now you do? And did you not then believe, and do you not still believe, that you were true members of Christ, though less perfect? Why then should you not judge of those that differ from you herein, as you judged of yourselves when you were as they now are? How needful then is it for Christians to distinguish (if ever they would be at peace and unity) between those truths which are essential to church-communion, and those that are not?

3. Unity and peace consists in all as with one shoulder practising and putting in execution the things we do know; Phil. iii. 16. "Nevertheless, whereto we have already attained, let us walk by the same rule, and mind the same thing." How sad is it to see our zeal consume us and our precious time in things doubtful and disputable, while we are not concerned nor affected with the practice of those indisputable things we all agree in! We all know charity to be the great command, and yet how few agree to practise it? We all know they that labour in the word and doctrine are worthy of double honour; and that God hath ordained, that they which preach the gospel should live of the gospel. These duties, however others have cavilled at them, I know you agree in them, and are persuaded of your duty therein: but where is your zeal to practise? O how well would it be with churches, if they were but half as zealous for the great, and plain, and indisputable things, and the more chargeable and costly things of religion, as they are for things doubtful or less necessary, or for things that are no charge to them, and cost them nothing but the breath of contention, though that may be too great a price for the small things they purchase with it!

But further, Do we not all agree, that men that preach the gospel should do it like workmen that need not be ashamed? and yet how little is this considered by many preachers, who never consider before they speak of what they say, or whereof they affirm! How few give themselves to study that they may be approved! How few meditate and give themselves to these things, that their profiting may appear to all!

For the Lord's sake let us unite to practise those things we know; and if we would have more talents, let us all agree to improve those we have.

See the spirit that was among the primitive professors, that knowing and believing how much it concerned them in the propagating of Christianity, to shew forth love to one another (that so all might know them to be Christ's disciples), rather than there should be any complainings among them, they sold all they had. O how zealous were these to practise, and as with one shoulder to do that that was upon their hearts for God! I might further add, how often have we agreed in our judgment? and hath it not been upon our hearts, that this and the other thing is good to be done, to enlighten the dark world, and to repair the breaches of churches, and to raise up those churches that now lie gasping, and among whom the soul of religion is expiring? But what do we more than talk of them? Do not most decline these things, when they either call for their purses or their persons to help in this and such like works as these? Let us then, in what we know, unite, that we may put it in practice, remembering, that if we know these things, we shall be happy if we do them.

4. This unity and peace consists in our joining and agreeing to pray for, and to press after, those truths we do not know. The disciples in the primitive times were conscious of their imperfections, and therefore they with one accord continued in prayer and supplications. If we were more in the sense of our ignorance and imperfections, we should carry it better towards those that differ from us: then we should abound more in the spirit of meekness and forbearance, that thereby we might bring others (or be brought by others) to the knowledge of the truth: this would make us go to God, and say with Elihu, Job xxxiv. 32, "That which we know not, teach thou us." Brethren, did we but all agree that we were erring in many things, we should soon agree to go to God, and pray for more wisdom and revelation of his mind and will concerning us.

But here is our misery, that we no sooner receive any thing for truth, but we presently ascend the chair of infallibility with it, as though in this we could not err: hence it is we are impatient of contradiction, and become uncharitable to those that are not of the same mind; but now a consciousness that we may mistake, or that if my brother err in one thing, I may err in another; this will unite us in affection, and engage us to press after perfection, according to that of the apostle; Phil. iii. 13–15, "Brethren, I count not myself to have apprehended: But this one thing I do, forgetting those things which are behind, and reaching forth unto those things which are before, I press toward the mark, for the prize of the high calling of God in Christ Jesus. And if in any thing ye be otherwise minded, God shall reveal even this unto you." O then that we could but unite and agree to go to God for one another, in confidence that he will teach us; and that if any one of us want wisdom (as who of us does not), we might agree to ask of God, who giveth to all men liberally, and upbraideth no man! Let us, like those people spoken of in the 2d of Isaiah, say to one another, "Come, let us go to the Lord, for he will teach us of his ways, and we will walk in his paths."

5. This unity and peace mainly consists in unity of love and affection: this is the great and indispensable duty of all Christians; by this they are declared Christ's disciples; And hence it is that love is called "the great commandment," "the old commandment," and "the new commandment;" that which was commanded in the beginning, and will remain to the end, yea, and after the end. 1 Cor. xiii. 8, "Charity never faileth; but whether there be tongues, they shall cease; or whether there be knowledge, it shall vanish away." And ver. 13, "And now abideth faith, hope, charity; but the greatest of these is charity." And Col. iii. 14, "Above all these things, put on charity, which is the bond of perfectness;" because charity is the end of the commandment, 1 Tim. i. 5. Charity is therefore called "the royal law;" as though it had a superintendency over other laws, and doubtless is a law to which other laws must give place, when they come in competition with it; "above all things, therefore, have fervent charity among yourselves; for charity shall cover the multitude of sins;" 1 Pet. iv. 8. Let us therefore live in unity and peace, and the God of love and peace will be with us.

That you may so do, let me remind you (in the words of a learned man), that the unity of the church is a unity of love and affection, and not a bare uniformity of practice and opinion.

III. Having shewn you wherein this unity consists, I now come to the third general thing propounded: and that is, to shew you the fruits and benefits of unity and peace, together with the mischiefs and inconveniences that attend those churches where unity and peace are wanting.

1. Unity and peace is a duty well-pleasing to God, who is styled the author of peace and not of confusion. In all the churches God's Spirit rejoiceth in the unity of our spirits; but on the other hand, where strife and divisions are, there the Spirit of God is grieved. Hence it is that the apostle no sooner calls upon the Ephesians not to grieve the Spirit of God, but he presently subjoins us a remedy against that evil, that they put away bitterness and evil-speaking,

and be kind one to another, and tender-hearted, forgiving one another, even as God for Christ's sake hath forgiven them; Eph. iv. 30, 32.

2. As unity and peace is pleasing to God, and rejoiceth his Spirit, so it rejoiceth the hearts and spirits of God's people. Unity and peace brings heaven down upon earth among us: hence it is that the apostle tells us, Rom. iv. 17, that "the kingdom of God is not meat and drink, but righteousness and peace and joy in the Holy Ghost." Where unity and peace is, there is heaven upon earth; by this we taste the first fruits of that blessed estate we shall one day live in the fruition of; when we shall come "to the general assembly and church of the first-born, whose names are written in heaven, and to God the judge of all, and to the spirits of just men made perfect;" Heb. xii. 23.

This outward peace of the church (as a learned man observes) distils into peace of conscience, and turns writings and readings of controversy into treatises of mortification and devotion.

And the Psalmist tells us, that it is not only good, but pleasant for brethren to dwell together in unity, Psalm cxxxiii. But where unity and peace is wanting, there are storms and troubles; "where envy and strife is, there is confusion and every evil work;" James iii. 16. It is the outward peace of the church that increaseth our inward joy; and the peace of God's house gives us occasion to eat our meat with gladness in our own houses, Acts ii. 46.

3. The unity and peace of the church makes communion of saints desirable. What is it that embitters church-communion, and makes it burdensome, but divisions? Have you not heard many complain, that they are weary of church-communion, because of church-contention? but now where unity and peace is, there Christians long for communion.

David saith, that he was glad when they said unto him, "Let us go to the house of God;" Psalm cxxii. 1. Why was this, but because (as the third verse tells us) Jerusalem was a city compact together, where the tribes went up, the tribes of the Lord, to give thanks to his name? And David, speaking of the man that was once his friend, doth thereby let us know the benefit of peace and unity; Psalm lv. 14. "We," saith he, "took sweet counsel together, and walked to the house of God in company." Where unity is strongest, communion is sweetest and most desirable. You see then that peace and union fills the people of God with desires after communion: but, on the other hand, hear how David complains, Psalm cxx., "Wo is me, that I sojourn in Mesech, and that I dwell in the tents of Kedar." The Psalmist here is thought to allude to a sort of men that dwelt in the deserts of Arabia, that got their livings by contention; and therefore he adds, ver. 6, that his soul had long dwelt with them that hated peace. This was that which made him long for the courts of God, and esteem one day in his house better than a thousand. This made his soul even faint for the house of God, because of the peace of it; "Blessed are they," saith he, "that dwell in thy house, they will be still praising thee." There is a certain note of concord, as appears, Acts ii., where we read of primitive Christians, meeting with one accord, praising God.

4. Where unity and peace is, there many mischiefs and inconveniences are prevented, which attend those people where peace and unity are wanting: and of those many that might be mentioned, I shall briefly insist upon these nine.

1. Where unity and peace is wanting, there is much precious time spent to no purpose. How many days are spent, and how many fruitless journeys made to no profit, where the people are not in peace? how often have many redeemed time (even in seed-time and harvest) when they could scarce afford it, to go to church, and, by reason of their divisions, come home worse than they went, repenting they have spent so much precious time to so little benefit? How sad is it to see men spend their precious time, in which they should work out their salvation, in labouring, as in the fire, to prove an uncertain and doubtful proposition, and to trifle away their time, in which they should make their calling and election sure, to make sure of an opinion, which, when they have done all, they are not infallibly sure whether it be true or no, because all things necessary to salvation and church-communion are plainly laid down in scripture, in which we may be infallibly sure of the truth of them; but for other things that we have no plain texts for, but the truth of them depends upon our interpretations, here we must be cautioned, that we do not spend much time in imposing those upon others, or venting those among others, unless we can assume infallibility, otherwise we spend time upon uncertainty. And whoever casts their eyes abroad, and do open their ears to intelligence, shall both see, and to their sorrow hear, that many churches spend most of their time in jangling and contending about those things which are neither essential to salvation nor church-communion; and that which is worse, about such doubtful questions which they are never able to give an infallible solution of. But now where unity and peace is, there our time is spent in praising God; and in those great questions, What we should do to be saved? and, How we may be more holy and more humble towards God, and more charitable and more serviceable to one another?

2. Where unity and peace is wanting, there is evil surmising and evil speaking, to the damage and disgrace, if not to the ruining, of one another; Gal. v. 14, 15. The whole law is fulfilled in one word, "Thou shalt love thy neighbour as thyself. But if you bite and devour one another, take heed you be not consumed one of another." No sooner the bond of charity is broken, which is as a wall about Christians, but soon they begin to make havock and spoil of one another; then there is raising evil reports, and taking up evil reports,

against each other. Hence it is that whispering and backbiting proceeds, and going from house to house to blazon the faults and infirmities of others: hence it is that we watch for the haltings of one another, and do inwardly rejoice at the miscarriages of others, saying in our hearts, "ha! ha! so we would have it:" but now where unity and peace is, there is charity; and where charity is, there we are willing to hide the faults, and cover the nakedness, of our brethren. "Charity thinketh no evil;" 1 Cor. xiii. 5; and therefore it cannot surmise, neither will it speak evil.

3. Where unity and peace is wanting, there can be no great matters enterprised—we cannot do much for God, nor much for one another; when the devil would hinder the bringing to pass of good in nations and churches, he divides their counsels (and as one well observes), he divides their heads, that he may divide their hands; when Jacob had prophesied of the cruelty of Simon and Levi, who were brethren, he threatens them with the consequent of it; Gen. xlix. 7, "I will divide them in Jacob, and scatter them in Israel." The devil is not to learn that maxim he hath taught the Machiavellians of the world, *Divide et impera*; divide and rule. It is an united force that is formidable. Hence the spouse in the Canticles is said to be but one, and the only one of her mother; Cant. vi. 9. Here upon it is said of her, ver. 10, "That she is terrible as an army with banners." What can a divided army do, or a disordered army that have lost their banners, or for fear or shame thrown them away? In like manner, what can Christians do for Christ, and the enlarging of his dominions in the world, in bringing men from darkness to light, while themselves are divided and disordered? Peace is to Christians as great rivers are to some cities, which (besides other benefits and commodities) are natural fortifications by reason whereof those places are made impregnable; but when, by the subtilty of an adversary or the folly of the citizens, these waters come to be divided into little petty rivulets, how soon are they assailed and taken? Thus it fares with churches, when once the devil or their own folly divides them, they will be so far from resisting of him, that they will be soon subjected by him.

Peace is to churches as walls to a city; nay, unity hath defended cities that had no walls. It was once demanded of Agesilaus, why Lacedemon had no walls; he answers (pointing back to the city), That the concord of the citizens was the strength of the city. In like manner, Christians are strong when united; then they are more capable to resist temptation, and to succour such as are tempted. When unity and peace is among the churches, then are they like a walled town; and when peace is the church's walls, salvation will be her bulwarks.

Plutarch tells us of one Silurus that had eighty sons, whom he calls to him as he lay upon his death-bed, and gave them a sheaf of arrows, thereby to signify, that if they lived in unity, they might do much, but if they divided, they would come to nothing. If Christians were all of one piece, if they were all but one lump, or but one sheaf or bundle, how great are the things they might do for Christ and his people in the world, whereas otherwise they can do little but dishonour him, and offend his!

It is reported of the leviathan, that his strength is in his scales; Job xli. 15–17, "His scales are his pride, shut up together as with a close seal; one is so near to another, that no air can come between them: they are joined together, they stick together, they cannot be sundered." If the church of God were united like the scales of the leviathan, it would not be every brain-sick notion, nor angry speculation, that would cause its separation.

Solomon saith, "Two are better than one," because, if one fall, the other may raise him; then surely twenty are better than two, and an hundred are better than twenty, for the same reason; because they are more capable to help one another. If ever Christians would do any thing to raise up the fallen tabernacles of Jacob, and to strengthen the weak, and comfort the feeble, and to fetch back those that have gone astray, it must be by unity.

We read of the men of Babel, Gen xi. 6, "The Lord said, Behold, the people are one, &c., and now nothing will be restrained from them that they have imagined to do."

We learn by reason, what great things may be done in worldly achievements where unity is; and shall not reason (assisted with the motives of religion) teach us, that unity among Christians may enable them to enterprise greater things for Christ? Would not this make Satan fall from heaven like lightning? For as unity built literal Babel, it is unity that must pull down mystical Babel. And, on the other hand, where divisions are, there is confusion; by this means a Babel hath been built in every age. It hath been observed by a learned man—and I wish I could not say truly observed—that there is most of Babel and confusion among those that cry out most against it.

Would we have a hand to destroy Babylon? let us have a heart to unite one among another.

Our English histories tell us, that after Austin the monk had been some time in England, he heard of some of the remains of the British Christians, which he convened to a place which Cambden in his Britannia calls "Austin's Oak." Here they met to consult about matters of religion; but such was their division, by reason of Austin's imposing spirit, that our stories tell us that synod was only famous for this, that they only met and did nothing. This is the mischief of divisions—they hinder the doing of much good; and if Christians that are divided be ever famous for any thing, it will be, that they have often met together, and talked of this and the other thing, but they did nothing.

4. Where unity and peace is wanting, there the weak are wounded, and the wicked are hardened. Unity may well be compared to precious oil, Psalm cxxxiii. 2. It is the nature of oil to heal that which is wounded, and to soften that which is hard. Those men that have hardened themselves against God, and his people, when they shall behold unity and peace among them, will say, God is in them indeed: and on the other hand, are they not ready to say, when they see you divided, That the devil is in you that you cannot agree!

5. Divisions and want of peace keep those out of the church that would come in; and cause many to go out that are in.

"The divisions of Christians (as a learned man observes) are a scandal to the Jews, an opprobrium to the Gentiles, and an inlet to atheism and infidelity:" insomuch that our controversies about religion (especially as they have been of late managed) have made religion itself become a controversy. O then, how good and pleasant a thing is it for brethren to dwell together in unity! The peace and unity that was among the primitive Christians drew others to them. What hinders the conversion of the Jews, but the divisions of Christians? Must I be a Christian? says the Jew. What Christian must I be? what sect must I be of? The Jews (as one observes), glossing upon that text in Isa. xi. 6, where it is prophesied, That the lion and the lamb shall lie down together, and that there shall be none left to hurt nor destroy in all God's holy mountain: they interpreting these sayings to signify the concord and peace that shall be among the people that shall own the Messiah, do from hence conclude, that the Messiah is not yet come, because of the contentions and divisions that are among those that profess him. And the apostle saith, 1 Cor. xiv. 23, that if an unbeliever should see their disorders, he would say they were mad; but where unity and peace is, there the churches are multiplied. We read, Acts ix., that when the churches had rest, they multiplied; and Acts ii. 46, 47, when the church was serving God with one accord, "the Lord added to them daily such as should be saved."

It is unity brings men into the church, and divisions keep them out. It is reported of an Indian, passing by the house of a Christian, and hearing them contending, being desired to turn in, he refused, saying, "Habamach dwells there," meaning that the devil dwelt there: but where unity and peace is, there God is; and he that dwells in love, dwells in God. The apostle tells the Corinthians, that if they walked orderly, even the unbelievers would hereby be enforced to come and worship, and say, God was in them indeed. And we read, Zech. viii. 23, of a time when ten men shall take hold of a Jew, and say, "We will go with you, for we have heard that God is with you."

And hence it is that Christ prays, John xvii. 21, that his disciples might be one, as the Father and he were one, that the world might believe the Father sent him: as if he should say, you may preach me as long as you will, and to little purpose, if you are not at peace and unity among yourselves. Such was the unity of Christians in former days, that the intelligent heathen would say of them, that though they had many bodies, yet they had but one soul. And we read the same of them, Acts iv. 32, that "the multitude of them that believed were of one heart and one soul."

And as the learned Stillingfleet observes in his Irenicum: "The unity and peace that was then among Christians made religion amiable in the judgment of impartial heathens: Christians were then known by the benignity and sweetness of their dispositions, by the candour and ingenuity of their spirits, by their mutual love, forbearance, and condescension to one another. But either this is not the practice of Christianity (viz., a duty that Christians are now bound to observe), or else it is not calculated for our meridian, where the spirits of men are of too high an elevation for it; for if pride and uncharitableness, if divisions and strifes, if wrath and envy, if animosities and contentions, were but the marks of true Christians, Diogenes need never light his lamp at noon to find out such among us; but if a spirit of meekness, gentleness, and condescension, if a stooping to the weaknesses and infirmities of one another, if pursuit after peace, when it flies from us, be the indispensable duties, and characteristical notes of Christians, it may possibly prove a difficult inquest to find out such among the crowds of those that shelter themselves under that glorious name."

It is the unity and peace of churches that brings others to them, and makes Christianity amiable. What is prophesied of the church of the Jews may in this case be applied to the Gentile church, Isa. lxvi. 12, that when once God extends peace to her like a river, the Gentiles shall come in like a flowing stream; then (and not till then) the glory of the Lord shall arise upon his churches, and his glory shall be seen among them; then shall their hearts fear and be enlarged, because the abundance of the nations shall be converted to them.

6. As want of unity and peace keeps those out of the church that would come in, so it hinders the growth of those that are in. Jars and divisions, wranglings and prejudices, eat out the growth, if not the life of religion. These are those waters of Marah, that embitter our spirits, and quench the Spirit of God. Unity and peace is said to be like the dew of Hermon, and as a dew that descended upon Sion, where the Lord commanded his blessing; Psalm cxxxiii. 3.

Divisions run religion into briars and thorns, contentions and parties. Divisions are to churches like wars in countries: where wars are, the ground lieth waste and untilled, none takes care of it. It is love that edifieth, but division pulleth down. Divisions are as the north-east wind to the fruits, which causeth them to dwindle away to nothing; but when the storms are over, every thing begins to grow. When men are divided, they seldom speak the truth in love; and then no marvel they grow not up to him in all things, who is the head.

It is a sad presage of an approaching famine (as one well observes), not of bread nor water, but of hearing the word of God, when the thin ears of corn devour the plump full ones; when the lean kine devour the fat ones; when our controversies about doubtful things, and things of less moment, eat up our zeal for the more indisputable and practical things in religion which may give us cause to fear, that this will be the character by which our age will be known to posterity—that it was the age that talked of religion most, and loved it least.

Look upon those churches where peace is, and there you shall find prosperity. When the churches had rest, they were not only multiplied, but, walking in the fear of the Lord and the comforts of the Holy Ghost, they were edified; it is when the whole body is knit together, as with joints and hands, that they increase with the increase of God.

We are at a stand sometimes, why there is so little growth among churches, why men have been so long in learning; and are yet so far from attaining the knowledge of the truth; some have given one reason, and some another; some say pride is the cause, and others say covetousness is the cause. I wish I could say these were no causes; but I observe, that when God entered his controversy with his people of old, he mainly insisted upon some one sin, as idolatry, and shedding innocent blood, &c., as comprehensive of the rest; not but that they were guilty of other sins, but those that were the most capital are particularly insisted on: in like manner, whoever would but take a review of churches that live in contentions and divisions, may easily find that breach of unity and charity is their capital sin, and the occasion of all other sins. No marvel then, that the Scripture saith, the whole law is fulfilled in love: and if so, then where love is wanting, it needs must follow the whole law is broken. It is where love grows cold that sin abounds; and therefore the want of unity and peace is the cause of that leanness and barrenness that is among us; it is true in spirituals as well as temporals, that peace brings plenty.

7. Where unity and peace is wanting, our prayers are hindered; the promise is, that what we shall agree to ask shall be given us of our heavenly Father: no marvel we pray and pray, and yet are not answered; it is because we are not agreed what to have.

It is reported that the people in Lacedemonia, coming to make supplication to their idol god, some of them asked for rain, and others of them asked for fair weather: the oracle returns them this answer, That they should go first and agree among themselves. Would a heathen god refuse to answer such prayers in which the supplicants were not agreed, and shall we think the true God will answer them?

We see then that divisions hinder our prayers, and lay a prohibition on our sacrifice: "If thou bring thy gift to the altar," saith Christ, "and there remember that thy brother hath aught against thee, leave thy gift, and go, and first be reconciled to thy brother, and then come and offer it." So that want of unity and charity hinders even our particular prayers and devotions.

This hindered the prayers and fastings of the people of old from finding acceptance; Isa. lviii. 3. The people ask the reason wherefore they fasted, and God did not see nor take notice of them. He gives this reason, Because they fasted for strife and debate, and hid their face from their own flesh. Again, Isa. lix., the Lord saith, his hand was not shortened, that he could not save; nor his ear heavy, that he could not hear: but their sins had separated between their God and them. And among those many sins they stood chargeable with, this was none of the least, viz., that the way of peace they had not known. You see where peace was wanting, prayers were hindered, both under the Old and New Testaments.

The sacrifice of the people, in the 65th of Isaiah, that said, "Stand by thyself, I am holier than thou," was a smoke in the nostrils of the Lord. On the other hand, we read how acceptable those prayers were that were made with one accord, Acts iv. 24, compared with verse 31. They prayed with one accord, and they were all of one heart, and of one soul: And see the benefit of it, "They were all filled with the Holy Ghost, and spoke the word with all boldness;" which was the very thing they prayed for, as appears verse 29. And the apostle exhorts the husband to dwell with his wife, that their prayers might not be hindered; 1 Pet. iii. 7. We see then want of unity and peace, either in families or churches, is a hinderance of prayers.

8. It is a dishonour and disparagement to Christ that his family should be divided. When an army falls into mutiny and division, it reflects disparagement on him that hath the conduct of it. In like manner, the divisions of families are a dishonour to the heads, and those that govern them. And if so, then how greatly do we dishonour our Lord and governor, who gave his body to be broken to keep his church from breaking, who prayed for their peace and unity, and left peace at his departing from them for a legacy, even a peace which the world could not bestow upon them.

9. Where there is peace and unity, there is a sympathy with each other; that which is the want of one will be the want of all. "Who is afflicted," saith the apostle, "and I burn not?" We should then "remember them that are in bonds, as bound with them; and them which suffer adversity, as being

ourselves also of the body;" Heb. xiii. 3. But where the body is broken, or men are not reckoned or esteemed of the body, no marvel we are so little affected with such as are afflicted. Where divisions are, that which is the joy of the one is the grief of another; but where unity and peace and charity abound, there we shall find Christians in mourning with them that mourn, and rejoicing with them that rejoice; then they will not envy the prosperity of others, nor secretly rejoice at the miseries or miscarriages of any.

IV. Last of all, I now come to give you twelve directions and motives for the obtaining peace and unity.

1. If ever we would live in peace and unity, we must pray for it. We are required to seek peace: of whom then can we seek it with expectation to find it, but of him who is a God of peace, and hath promised to bless his people with peace? It is God that hath promised to give his people one heart, and one way; yet for all these things he will be sought unto: O then let us seek peace, and pray for peace, because God shall prosper them that love it.

The peace of churches is that which the apostle prays for in all his epistles; in which his desire is, that grace and peace may be multiplied and increased among them.

2. They that would endeavour the peace of the churches, must be careful who they commit the care and oversight of the churches to; as (1.)—Over and besides those qualifications that should be in all Christians, they that rule the church of God should be men of counsel and understanding. Where there is an ignorant ministry, there is commonly an ignorant people, according as it was of old—Like priest like people.

How sad is it to see the church of God committed to the care of such that pretend to be teachers of others, that understand not what they say, or whereof they affirm. No marvel the peace of churches is broken, when their watchmen want skill to preserve their unity, which of all other things is as the church's walls; when they are divided, no wonder they crumble to atoms, if there is no skilful physician to heal them. It is sad when there is no balm in Gilead, and when there is no physician there. Hence it is, that the wounds of churches become incurable, like the wounds of God's people of old, either not healed at all, or else slightly healed, and to no purpose. May it not be said of many churches this day, as God said of the church of Israel, That he sought for a man among them that should stand in the gap, and make up the breach; but he found none?

Remember what was said of old, Mal. ii. 7, The priest's lips preserve knowledge: and the people should seek the law at his mouth. But when this is wanting, the people will be stumbling, and departing from God and one another; therefore God complains, Hos. iv. 6, That his people were destroyed for want of knowledge; that is, for want of knowing guides; for if the light that is in them that teach be darkness, how great is that darkness! and if the blind lead the blind, no marvel both fall into the ditch.

How many are there that take upon them to teach others, that had need be taught in the beginning of religion; that instead of multiplying knowledge, multiply words without knowledge; and instead of making known God's counsel, darken counsel by words without knowledge? The apostle speaks of some that did more than darken counsel; for they wrested the counsel of God; 2 Pet. iii. 16. In Paul's epistles, saith he, "are some things hard to be understood, which they that are unlearned and unstable wrest, as they do also the other scriptures, to their own destruction." Some things in the Scriptures are hard to be known, and they are made harder by such unlearned teachers as utter their own notions by words without knowledge.

None are more bold and adventurous to take upon them to expound the dark mysteries and sayings of the prophets and Revelations, and the 9th of the Romans, which I believe contains some of those many things which, in Paul's epistles, Peter saith, were "hard to be understood;" I say none are more forward to dig in these mines than those that can hardly give a sound reason for the first principles of religion; and such as are ignorant of many more weighty things that are easily to be seen in the face and superficies of the Scripture; nothing will serve these but swimming in the deeps, when they have not yet learned to wade through the shallows of the Scriptures: like the Gnosticks of old, who thought they knew all things, though they knew nothing as they ought to know. And as those Gnosticks did of old, so do such teachers of late break the unity and peace of churches.

How needful then is it, that if we desire the peace of churches, that we choose out men of knowledge, who may be able to keep them from being shattered and scattered with every wind of doctrine: and who may be able to convince and stop the mouths of gainsayers.

(2.) You must not only choose men of counsel, but if you would design the unity and peace of the churches, you must choose men of courage to govern them; for as there must be wisdom to hear with some, so there must be courage to correct others: as some must be instructed meekly, so others must be rebuked sharply, that they may be sound in the faith; there must be wisdom to rebuke some within long-suffering, and there must be courage to suppress and stop the mouths of others. The apostle tells Titus of some whose mouths must be stopped, or else they would subvert whole houses, Titus i. 11. Where this courage hath been wanting, not only whole houses, but whole churches have been subverted. And Paul tells the Galatians, that when he saw some endeavour to bring the churches into bondage, that he did not give place to them, no not for an hour, &c, Gal. ii. 5. If this course had been taken by the rulers of churches, their peace had not been so often invaded by unruly and vain talkers.

3. In choosing men to rule (if you would endeavour to keep the unity of the Spirit, and the bond of peace thereby), be careful you choose men of peaceable dispositions. That which hath much annoyed the peace of churches hath been the froward and perverse spirits of the rulers thereof. Solomon therefore adviseth, That with a furious man we should not go, lest we learn his ways, and get a snare to our souls, Prov. xxii. 24, 25, and with the froward we learn frowardness. How do some men's words eat like a canker; who instead of lifting up their voices like a trumpet to sound a parley for peace, have rather sounded an alarm to war and contention. If ever we would live in peace, let us reverence the feet of them that bring the glad tidings of it.

O how have some men made it their business to preach contentions, and upon their entertainment of every novel opinion to preach separation! How hath God's word been stretched and torn to furnish these men with arguments to tear churches! Have not our ears heard those texts that say, "Come out from among them, and be separate," &c., and "Withdraw from every brother that walks disorderly?" I say, have we not heard these texts that were written to prevent disorder brought to countenance the greatest disorder that ever was in the church of God, even schism and division? whereas one of these exhortations was written to the church of Corinth to separate themselves from the idol's temple, and the idol's table, in which many of them lived in the participation of, notwithstanding their profession of the true God; as appears, 2 Cor. vi. 1.6, 17, compared with 1 Cor. viii. 7, and as 1 Cor. x. 14, 20, 22, recites; and not for some few or more members, who shall make themselves both judges and parties to make separation, when and as often as they please, from the whole congregation and church of God, where they stood related; for by the same rule, and upon the same ground, may others start some new question among these new separatists, and become their own judges of the communicableness of them, and thereupon make another separation from these, till at last two be not left to walk together. And for that other text mentioned, 2 Thess. iii. 6, where Paul exhorts the church of Thessalonica to withdraw themselves from every brother that walks disorderly; I cannot but wonder that any should bring this to justify their separation or withdrawal from the communion of a true (though a disorderly) church. For,

(1.) Consider, that this was not writ for a few members to withdraw from the church, but for the church to withdraw from disorderly members.

(2.) Consider, that if any offended members, upon pretence of error, either in doctrine or practice, should by this text become judges (as well as parties)

of the grounds and lawfulness of their separation; then it will follow, that half a score notorious heretics, or scandalous livers (when they have walked so as they forsee the church are ready to deal with them, and withdraw from them), shall anticipate the church, and pretend somewhat against them, of which themselves must be judges, and so withdraw from the church, pretending either heresy or disorder; and so condemn the church, to prevent the disgrace of being condemned by the church. How needful then is it, that men of peaceable dispositions, and not of froward and fractious and dividing spirits, be chosen to rule the church of God, for fear lest the whole church be leavened and soured by them!

4. As there must be care used in choosing men to rule the church of God, so there must be a consideration had, that there are many things darkly laid down in scripture; this will temper our spirits, and make us live in peace and unity the more firmly in things in which we agree; this will help us to bear one another's burdens, and so fulfil the law of Christ, inasmuch as all things necessary to salvation and church communion are plainly laid down in scripture. And where things are more darkly laid down, we should consider that God intended hereby to stir up our diligence, that thereby we might increase our knowledge, and not our divisions, for it may be said of all discoveries of truth we have made in the Scriptures, as it is said of the globe of the earth, that though men have made great searches, and thereupon great discoveries, yet there is still a *terra incognita*, an unknown land; so there is in the Scriptures: for after men have travelled over them, one age after another, yet still there is, as it were, a *terra incognita*, an unknown track to put us upon farther search and inquiry, and to keep us from censuring and falling out with those who have not yet made the same discoveries; that so we may say with the Psalmist, when we reflect upon our short apprehensions of the mind of God, that we have seen an end of all perfection, but God's commands are exceeding broad; and as one observes, speaking of the Scriptures, that there is a path in them leading to the mind of God, which lieth a great distance from the thoughts and apprehensions of men. And on the other hand, in many other places, God sits, as it were, on the superficies, and the face of the letter, where he that runs may discern him speaking plainly, and no parable at all. How should the consideration of this induce us to a peaceable deportment towards those that differ!

5. If we would endeavour peace and unity, we must consider how God hath tempered the body, that so the comely parts should not separate from the uncomely, as having no need of them; 1 Cor. xii. 23–25. There is in Christ's body and house some members and vessels less honourable; 2 Tim. ii. 20. And therefore we should not, as some now-a-days do, pour the more abundant disgrace, instead of putting the more abundant honour upon them. Did we but consider this, we should be covering the weakness, and

hiding the miscarriages of one another, because we are all members one of another, and the most useless member in his place is useful.

6. If we would live in peace, let us remember our relations to God, as children to a father, and to each other as brethren. Will not the thoughts that we have one Father, quiet us; and the thoughts that we are brethren, unite us? It was this that made Abraham propose terms of peace to Lot; Gen. xiii, "Let there be no strife," saith he, "between us, for we are brethren." And we read of Moses, in Acts vii. 26, using this argument to reconcile those that strove together, and to set them at one again: "Sirs," saith he, "you are brethren, why do you wrong one another?" A deep sense of this relation, that we are brethren, would keep us from dividing.

7. If we would preserve peace, let us mind the gifts and graces and virtues that are in each other; let these be more in our eye than their failings and imperfections. When the apostle exhorted the Philippians to peace, as a means hereunto, that so the peace of God might rule in their hearts, he tells them, iv. 8, "That if there were any virtue, or any praise, they should think of these things." While we are always talking and blazoning the faults of one another, and spreading their infirmities, no marvel we are so little in peace and charity; for as charity covereth a multitude of sins, so malice covereth a multitude of virtues, and makes us deal by one another, as the heathen persecutors dealt with Christians, viz., put them in bears' skins, that they might the more readily become a prey to those dogs that were designed to devour them.

8. If we would keep unity and peace, let us lay aside provoking and dividing language, and forgive those that use it. Remember that old saying, "Evil words corrupt good manners." When men think to carry all before them, with speaking uncharitably and disgracefully of their brethren or their opinions, may not such be answered as Job answered his unfriendly visitants, Job vi. 25, "How forcible are right words; but what doth your arguing reprove?" How healing are words fitly spoken? A word in season, how good is it? If we would seek peace, let us clothe all our treaties for peace with acceptable words; and where one word may better accommodate than another, let that be used to express persons or things by; and let us not, as some do, call the different practices of our brethren, will-worship, and their different opinions, doctrines of devils, and the doctrine of Balaam, who taught fornication, &c., unless we can plainly, and in expressness of terms, prove it so. Such language as this hath strangely divided our spirits, and hardened our hearts one towards another.

9. If we would live in peace, let us make the best constructions of one another's words and actions. Charity judgeth the best, and it thinks no evil; if words and actions may be construed to a good sense, let us never put a

bad construction upon them. How much hath the peace of Christians been broken by an uncharitable interpretation of words and actions? As some lay to the charge of others that which they never said, so, by straining men's words, others lay to their charge that they never thought.

10. Be willing to hear, and learn, and obey those that God by his providence hath set over you; this is a great means to preserve the unity and peace of churches: but when men (yea, and sometimes women) shall usurp authority, and think themselves wiser than their teachers, no wonder if these people run into contentions and parties, when any shall say they are not free to hear those whom the church thinks fit to speak to them. This is the first step to schism, and is usually attended, if not timely prevented, with a sinful separation.

11. If you would keep the unity of the spirit in the bond of peace, be mindful, that the God whom you serve is a God of peace, and your Saviour is a Prince of peace, and that "his ways are ways of pleasantness, and all his paths are peace;" and that Christ was sent into the world "to give light to them that sit in darkness, and in the shadow of death, and to guide our feet in the way of peace."

12. Consider the oneness of spirit that is among the enemies of religion; though they differ about other things, yet to persecute religion, and extirpate religion out of the earth, here they will agree; the devils in the air, and the devils in the earth, all the devils in hell, and in the world, make one at this turn. Shall the devil's kingdom be united; and shall Christ's be divided? Shall the devils make one shoulder to drive on the design of damning men, and shall not Christians unite to carry on the great design of saving of them? Shall the papists agree and unite to carry on their interest, notwithstanding the multitudes of orders, degrees, and differences, that are among them; and shall not those that call themselves reformed churches, unite to carry on the common interest of Christ in the world, notwithstanding some petty and disputable differences that are among them? Quarrels about religion (as one observes) were sins not named among the Gentiles. What a shame is it then for Christians to abound in them, especially considering the nature of the Christian religion, and what large provisions the Author of it hath made, to keep the profession's of it in peace! insomuch (as one well observes), it is next to a miracle that ever any (especially the professors of it) should fall out about it.

13. Consider and remember, that the Judge stands at the door. Let this moderate your spirits, that the Lord is at hand. What a sad account will they have to make when he comes, that shall be found to smite their fellow-servants, and to make the way to his kingdom more narrow than ever he made it! Let me close all in the words of that great apostle, 2 Cor. xiii. 11,

"Finally, brethren, farewell. Be perfect, be of good comfort, be of one mind, live in peace, and the God of love and peace shall be with you."

Postscript.—Reader, I thought good to advertise thee, that I have delivered this to thy hand in the same order and method in which it was preached, and almost in the same words, without any diminishings or considerable enlargings, unless it be in the thirteen last particulars; upon some of which I have made some enlargements, which I could not then do for want of time; but the substance of every one of them was then laid down in the same particular order as here thou hast them. And now I have done, I make no other account (to use the words of a moderate man upon the like occasion) but it will fall out with me, as doth commonly with him that parts a fray, both parties may perhaps drive at me for wishing them no worse than peace. My ambition of the public tranquillity of the church of God, I hope, will carry me through these hazards; let both beat me, so their quarrels may cease, I shall rejoice in those blows and scars I shall take for the church's safety.

Milton Keynes UK
Ingram Content Group UK Ltd.
UKHW011600110124
435868UK00004B/460

9 789355 340832